Lea ... ch

What Can We Lea... Those Who Are Done with Church?

Robin Stockitt

Rector, St James, Donemana,
Diocese of Derry and Raphoe, Northern Ireland

S John Dawson

Formerly Teacher and Hospital Chaplain

GROVE BOOKS LIMITED

RIDLEY HALL RD CAMBRIDGE CB3 9HU

Contents

First Impression June 2020
ISSN 0144-171X
ISBN 978 1 78827 126 4

Meet the Donewiths

1

Leaving Church: A Memoir of Faith is the title of a book originally published in 2006 in which the author, Barbara Brown Taylor, describes her decision to leave her job after fifteen years as a full-time Episcopal priest. In an interview she highlights the tensions of her religious life, in particular that of receiving a salary as a 'professional holy person' for *loving people*. It was at the point in which her church had 'succeeded' by doubling in membership, budget and the number of services, that she felt that her work for God was taking her away from God. She no longer wanted to be 'set apart,' as they referred to ordination, and felt that the holiest thing she could be was the flawed human being God had made her to be. She explains how she increasingly came to believe that if her job were to support church members as they engaged in vocations in the world, then what sense did it make to locate that person inside the four safe walls of a church? She preferred to see herself 'like one of those libraries on wheels that goes wherever people need books…My heart belonged in the world. I belonged among the laity, not the clergy.' Her decision to leave church (she told a clergy friend) was not because she had lost her faith. If anything, she said, 'it was a bid to live into that faith more fully.'

Towards the end of the book Barbara Brown Taylor asks a series of searching questions: 'What if people were invited (to church) to come tell what they already know of God instead of to learn what they are supposed to believe? What if they were blessed for what they are doing in the world instead of chastened for not doing more at church? What if church felt more like a way-station than a destination? What if the church's job were to move people out of the door instead of trying to keep them in, by convincing them that God needed them more in the world than in the church?' Once she had left the church, she said, 'I renewed my membership in the priesthood of all believers, who may not have as much power as we would like, but whose consolation prize is the freedom to meet God after work, well away from all centres of religious command, *wherever God shows up*.'

> The only thing I want, says the Lord, are people with humble and contrite hearts, people who observe my ways. In the presence of those people I will make my home. (Isa 66.1–2)

There is seemingly a growing number of Christians who similarly feel that they are 'done with' church. These people are usually those who have been the most committed and active members of their congregations, and it is not because they have abandoned their faith or given up on God. Michael Fanstone, in his book *The Sheep That Got Away*, reported that only 7% of church-leavers he surveyed pointed to 'God issues' as their reason for leaving church—this included both a loss of faith but also the development of a view of God which was not reflected in the church they left.[1] They continue to see their Christian faith as central to their lives but feel that those lives can best be served outside of the institutional church. They still believe that they are part of the body of Christ, they continue to meet with other Christians for fellowship, to study the Bible and to pray, but they no longer want to be a part of the established church. Described as 'the fastest growing denomination—Christians who do not go to church,' many even come from clergy who have been in the ministry for several decades.

About this Study

The aim of this booklet is to explore this phenomenon—why so many followers of Christ no longer attend church. Furthermore, is this actually a cause for concern and is the reaction of the institutional church helping or hindering? Could it really be that this movement has been provoked by God?

> **Why do so many followers of Christ no longer attend church?**

To assist in this process we have been able to interview a representative group of these people who were once very involved in the life of their churches but, although they have not abandoned their faith, simply no longer have a desire to attend. It would be true to say that encountering so many of these people was the catalyst for embarking upon this project. In a relatively small geographical area a large number of Christians emerged who had this shared experience. In turn, they were able to signpost others who were in an almost identical situation. Their ages ranged from early 40s to late 70s, with the majority being in the late 50s/early 60s bracket. They all, from a variety of church backgrounds—Anglican, Baptist, free church etc—expressed a willingness to talk about their experiences.

Interviews lasted anything from one to three hours and, while some wanted very direct questions to be asked, others preferred to talk generally about their situation, although this almost inevitably covered the same ground. The sequence of questioning began with an account of how they had initially been introduced into the life of the church, what that had meant to them and what their involvement had been. Then they were asked whether there had been a particular turning point that triggered their departure or whether it had been a gradual process. Did it then seem strange to be out of the church attending routine, and did they feel there was a gap that needed to be filled? Then there was an exploration of the effect that leaving church had had on their relationship with God and other believers, and how this had evolved over time. Their ongoing relationship with church was then considered (*eg* whether they foresaw a time that they might return to the established church and if the church they had left had got in touch with them), before then looking at whether they thought the established church was operating in the way Jesus would have wanted it to. This final area of discussion was left open-ended and certainly provoked the lengthiest and most significant comments.

The majority of those interviewed had spent most of their lives involved in church, often from a very early age, since that was common for their particular generation. Sunday school, youth clubs, and youth camps regularly featured as they described their background. A few had come to faith later in life and spoke about a conversion experience, which had then led to involvement in church life. Almost all of them spoke of expectations placed upon them as they took on various roles and responsibilities within their church. One very definite expectation was that attendance at church services was almost non-negotiable; it was what was expected of them. Although they found some aspects of church difficult, citing examples such as the demands on their time when they were already trying to balance work and family commitments, none of those interviewed had considered not going to church at that stage of their lives—they believed that it was what God wanted them to do, although they had always felt that church itself was secondary to their personal relationship with God.

Almost all of those interviewed were far more than church attenders. They spoke of commitments to pastoring, teaching, leading home groups and youth groups, tithing, networking and music. They had participated fully in a faith community for all the reasons that are given for continuing participation: fellowship, worship, teaching, service, accountability and so on. But now, for a variety of reasons, they were looking elsewhere to meet their needs. None was actually involvxed in paid ministry (although one was the wife of a minister) but they must all have been an enormous help and support to the leader(s) of their churches. Almost without exception their commitment and willingness to serve in this way were unwavering; they were certainly not self-serving, lazy or apathetic. They were the very people who would be most likely to be finding their needs for personal spiritual growth satisfied by their involvement with the church. They certainly did not want to do away with church or

To an increasing degree the church has been losing its best

parachurch; but they found themselves in the gap between the ideals of the New Testament and the realities of actual groups of Christians.

To an increasing degree the church has been losing its best—the very people on whom a church relies for service, lay leadership and financial support are leaving and they are not looking to be won back. Nor, which exacerbates this situation, are the younger people in the next generation coming through to fill their seats.

From Church-goer to Church-gone

2

So, what happens in the lives of these committed Christians, unwavering in their faith and seeking to get closer to God, that provokes them to leave the institution of the church to which they have been committed and in which they have served, often for several decades? Why is it that not only do such people rarely abandon faith altogether, but frequently claim that leaving the church is actually a way of maintaining their faith?

Very few of those interviewed spoke of a sudden decision to leave their church or, for example, a single catastrophic incident. There was not an identifiable falling-out; instead, in the vast majority of cases it was a gradual process, a cumulative effect—time spans of up to two years were mentioned. People seem to 'drift away,' as C S Lewis described it. Just as spirituality is a process, disillusionment with the church (or the faith) is a process too. It does not seem to happen overnight. Some spoke of a feeling of disconnect, feeling invisible (particularly in the case of single people) and spending a lot of time trying to figure out where they fitted in, even though they had often been attending the church for twenty to thirty years. Steve Aisthorpe, in his book *The Invisible Church*, describes this feeling as 'a perceived deficit of love.'[2] Others who spoke of this cumulative effect had wanted to stay and to work through things. They had still believed in the value of the Christian community, at least in the ideal. Sadly, their decision was often prompted by the perceived hypocrisy and behaviour of other members of the church and, in particular, church leaders. Church leaders were criticized for being authoritarian, for heavy shepherding, and for issues of control, and there were real concerns about what was called the 'professional priesthood' and the concept of paid ministry. A common concern was that this often led to an introspective view of church and its institutions, a consequence of which is that straightforward relationships are often sacrificed to protect the system.

Disillusionment with the church does not seem to happen overnight

It seems a sad reflection that so many spoke of feeling worse on leaving the church building each Sunday than they had on entering, often because those at the front were implicitly suggesting that sinless perfection was possible this side of heaven. They had become increasingly disillusioned and, in the words of one person, 'Going to church actually started to leave me with an incredible sense of sadness. Church has lost the core of its being. It's all surface—surface teaching, surface preaching and people living a façade.'

Almost without exception those interviewed viewed their decision to leave church as something they felt had been provoked by God; one person used the metaphor of being derailed by God in preparation for being re-routed in a better direction. There was a feeling that one day we might look back on this time as one when God was acting to bring about the kind of historic transformation that we seem to see every few centuries.

Change in Routines

In the vast majority of cases we were dealing with Christians who had attended church regularly on a Sunday morning for most of their long lives. What seemed particularly surprising was that, with one exception, nobody found it strange to be out of the routine of church attendance. In fact they referred to it as being 'good' or a 'relief' to be out of that. One person said that it had taken a while to 'sidestep guilt' but she had had no problem with leaving and it had been beneficial spiritually to be in a quiet space with just herself and God. Maybe, after all, Jesus is looking for more than well-attended church services, even though our current model seems directed at this and little else.

Being out of the (often longstanding) routine of church involvement and attendance would suggest that there was now a gap to be filled, if for no other reason than a time issue. None of the respondents saw it that way and were quick to talk about that time being filled with 'God-time'; furthering their relationship with God or, in some cases, with other Christian communities. Maybe this partly explains why attendance at cathedrals is up 14% in the last decade; the cathedral offers an experience without a commitment. In some cases it was felt that time had actually been freed up to get more involved in community action and to explore what God wanted to do through them. In fact there was an overwhelming sense that this action had strengthened their relationship with God as they discovered that it was not based on church and Sundays. Richard Rohr puts it this way, 'I feel that people facing important issues of social justice, divorce, failure, gender identity, an inner life of prayer, or a radical reading of the gospel are usually bored and limited by the typical Sunday church agenda. And these are good people. But they keep on doing what Bill Plotkin calls their survival dance[3] because no-one has told them about their sacred dance.'

They discovered that their relationship with God was not based on church and Sundays

With regards to relationships with other believers, there was a sense that, if anything, stronger bonds had been developed as all of those interviewed continued to meet on a regular basis with other Christians for prayer and Bible study as well as socially. Looking at people's experiences of leaving congregations, one of the striking things is their hunger for fellowship. Indeed, having left a traditional congregation, the first thing many do is to seek out opportunities for meeting with other believers. Most described how they had formed friendships or linked into informal groups which had Christian fellowship as an important part of their purpose. There was a real feeling that the most meaningful corporate activities happened outside of the church buildings with people whom one described as 'life-joints.' Above all, they wanted to have church where people were more authentic. As Tim Chester put it in his book, *A Meal with Jesus: Discovering Grace, Community and Mission Around the Table*, 'This is what the church is to be: a community of broken people finding family around a meal under the tree of Calvary.'[4]

One of the questions posed to interviewees was whether they foresaw a time when they might return to the institutional church. Nobody ruled this out but it was not something they were currently considering. Circumstances, many felt, may ultimately dictate this decision (*eg* if a partner took an interest) but this would be more about a feature of their experience than a need to belong.

Christ-like Church?

The question that most exercised the thoughts of those interviewed was whether they thought that the established church was operating the way that Jesus would have wanted it to. Three areas were consistently raised when this was asked. First, the issues of performance and presentation, whether relating to what came from the pulpit, especially against the background of pomp and ceremony and the perceived clash between the kingdom of God and human empires, or that of worship leaders and where the real focus should be. They related to what Francis Chan said in his book, *Letters to the Church,* 'The early church didn't need energetic music, great videos, attractive leaders or elaborate lighting to be excited about being part of God's body. The pure gospel was enough to put them in a place of awe…In our arrogance we created something we think works better.'[5] Martin Lloyd-Jones commented in a similar vein: 'When the church is absolutely different from the world, she invariably attracts it. It is then that the world is made to listen to her message, though it may hate it at first.'[6]

Fellowship and relationships were not valued as highly as they should be

Secondly, there was a feeling that true fellowship and relationships were not valued as highly as they should be. And thirdly, there was a sense that churches were far too introverted and failed to serve their community the way that they should. Celebrity culture and incessant entertainment were cited as obstacles when what they wanted was to worship Jesus and to encourage one another without all the worldly rigmarole. 'Perhaps more than anything else, what people want out of a church is a community of people who are experiencing God together.'[7]

One of the most surprising responses, especially when we consider the fact that many of those interviewed had been attending a particular church for many years, was when they were asked if the church had made any attempt to get in touch after they had left. With one exception—and that related to an administrative detail relating to church membership—they said that they had had no meaningful contact. In their book *Gone for Good,* Leslie Francis and Philip J Richter found that, in the case of 92% of leavers, no-one from the church had talked to them about why they had ceased to attend.[8] In fact, the onus seemed to have fallen on those who had left to request an opportunity to explain their position. Experience shows that there is a six to eight week window of time during which they wait for someone from church to contact them. They want someone to listen, and to know whether they are even missed. If no-one contacts within that period they move on.

In William P Young's best-selling 2007 novel, *The Shack,* Mack's views of the church are challenged: 'Mack, that's because you're only seeing the institution, a man-made system. That's not what I came to build. What I see are people and their lives, a living breathing community of all those who love me, not buildings and programmes...It's all about relationships and simply sharing life. My church is all about people and life is all about relationships...As well intended as it might be, you know that religious machinery can chew up people. An awful lot of what is done in my name has nothing to do with me and is often, even if unintentional, very contrary to my purposes...I don't create institutions—never have, never will.'[9]

Factors in Leaving

It seems that there are many reasons and provocations for believers to become Donewiths. It has been fairly easy to compile a list of the frustrations that emerge although, in most cases, it will not be any of the following in isolation. The Donewiths' decision is usually as a result of a combination of several factors:

- A weariness with the internal politics of churches, which can lead to infighting, gossip and doctrinal conflict.
- The power struggles and the abuse of power. Who is it that makes decisions and who is it that exerts pressure to sway how those decisions are made?

- The lack of application and relevance to the very real and pressing issues of daily life.
- The gap between what is proclaimed and the actuality of people's lives, leading to the feeling that the church has become a place of hypocrisy and judgmentalism.
- Tired of being a passive audience and of being subject to pressures to conform to leadership expectations, in order to comply with an acceptable model.
- Too much teaching that at the root has one basic message—'You must do better!' in areas such as being better witnesses or being more committed.
- The constant requirement to commit time, money, effort and goods to projects that are not necessarily in line with their own convictions and gifting, and frequently at the expense of their own identity in Christ.
- Living in a performance culture that defines what is a good Christian, thereby tacitly encouraging a cycle of works rather than the cycle of grace.
- Anti-intellectualism by which church leaders make clear their distrust of science or history, if it conflicts with their own message.
- A lack of compassion and genuine pastoral care.
- Questionable use of finances, and lack of accountability in this area.
- Praise and worship that is too much of a performance and no longer inspiring towards God.
- Becoming bored with the ritual, routine and the 'same-old' of church.

If these are the specific issues that those interviewed mentioned, then it is necessary now to illustrate how these frustrations might have arisen and to ask what lies beneath the surface.

3 Reading the Signs

Being able to stand in the shoes of another is the essence of empathy. Seeing the world through the eyes of someone else and being able to enter into their emotional responses is our task if we are truly to listen to those who have chosen to leave their churches after many years of involvement. One way of doing that, perhaps, is by reading the signs—church signs. This is no simple task. Words are slippery things and refuse to sit tidily on one page in a dictionary. The reason for this is that words have invisible hooks attached to them eliciting associations and emotional responses drawn from the well of our own experience. Take for example the world 'family.' For some this immediately evokes warm and fuzzy memories of bedtime stories, playing with Grandad in the garden and idyllic holidays on the beach. Yet for others, family means danger, bewilderment and abuse. This is why church mottos can both inspire and repel. The critiques that follow are an attempt to view church mission statements with the eyes of those who might be teetering on the edge of belonging to a local congregation.

In a town near where I live (population 61,000) there are 53 churches, each offering their own version of faith for possible new customers. Every one has its own flavour and unique selling point. Some look grey and austere from the outside, conveying an unspoken message that the Christian faith is an extremely serious business, with little room for creativity or colour. Others are bright and cheerful, suggesting that the journey of faith is fun and sparkly.

Perhaps most revealing of all are the mission statements that articulate in a few words what the essence of a church is all about. This chapter will take just four of these and attempt to assess the theological assumptions that underpin them. It is these presuppositions that determine the shape of a church's corporate life together, and this is perhaps where the dissatisfaction, which Donewiths feel so acutely, originates. Let us take some examples.

Serving Christ, Serving Others

This sign is emblazoned across a building in a nearby town. At first glance this sounds thoroughly biblical and entirely worthy. Who could possibly disagree with such a sentiment? A lifetime of service beckons for those who choose to join this church. But for those souls who are wrestling with questions of belief and doubt, with issues of belonging or distancing, with mystery as well as certainty, I wonder if such a simple message could provoke a sense of unease. Such people have begun to feel that belonging to a church has become like wearing clothes that belong to someone else. The size is not right, nor the colour, nor the texture. This collar is chafing at the neck and the shoes have holes in their soles.

What might these people think of such a slogan? They might ask, 'Did not Jesus explicitly say, "I no longer call you servants, because a servant does not know his master's business. Instead, I have called you friends"?' In this text Jesus is intent on reframing his disciples' sense of identity. Jesus asserts that we are not to think of our relationship with God in terms of servant and master, for such a depiction is insufficiently intimate. From now on we are to see ourselves in an entirely different light. Being a friend of Jesus defines our truest and deepest identity; being a servant of Jesus describes merely our actions and activities. The God that this motto proclaims could sound like a God who is most impressed by service, rather than by the quality and closeness of relationship with us. Is such a God someone I want to get to know?

But one might press this interrogation further. There is an implicit hierarchy here with service to Christ coming first, serving others second and attentiveness to one's own individual needs, longings and anxieties nowhere to be seen at all. It suggests that to be attentive to our own interior world, our own inner landscape is not even worth mentioning. For those who are Donewiths, this encapsulates where the rub lies. What if I have doubts and questions about God? What if I want to learn to play the piano? What about my daughter who appears to be swayed by her peers rather too easily? What on Earth can I do about that really irritating colleague at work? What about all these things that are the stuff of my life, yet do not seem to fall into either category of serving Christ and serving others? Where is the me in that sentence? And does the absence of me signify that it is of less importance than anything else?

And lastly, what on earth do we mean by service? For relationships between two people to be truly enriching there must surely be elements of mutuality, reciprocity, kindness and hospitality. Service, by contrast, implies that there is a giver and a recipient. The giver might decide that a particular person is in need of service, that they are needy. Immediately an unequal asymmetrical relationship is established with the giver taking on the unasked-for role of rescuer.

So this simple four-word mission statement could be read as:

- Having a theology of the nature of God that is defined in terms of performance rather than relationship.

- Having a theology of the self that is minimized if not actually excised altogether.
- Having an emphasis on being busy as something of great value, as opposed to the importance of a lifestyle which is more open to reflection and contemplation.

These theological underpinnings might be felt more than they are actually articulated and for someone who is teetering on the edge of belonging to a church they could easily become a Donewith.

We Exist to Make Heaven More Crowded

What are the theological assumptions that underpin this mission statement? At first glance it sounds exciting and positive. A crowded heaven, with saved souls rejoicing together for all eternity. And by contrast a depopulated hell. The main focus of this church is to urge and equip its members to evangelize, as this is considered to be the primary activity of being a disciple of Christ.

On closer examination, however, it makes a clear statement that this present world and our contemporary lives are of secondary importance compared to the eternal destiny of souls after death. It is the afterlife that matters most, not the here and now. Whilst the emphasis is clearly on heaven, the lurking shadow of eternal separation from God, if not actual conscious torment, should be enough to impel the members of this church to a lifestyle of continuous intentional evangelism.

For someone struggling with church, as Donewiths are, the Lord's Prayer might come to mind. Does the prayer not say, 'Your kingdom come, your will be done, on Earth as it is in heaven'? This prayer seems to present an entirely alternative vista to the church motto. This prayer is about now, about this Earth, this life, my existence and the urgent petition is that something of the flavour and texture of heaven could be found on Earth right now. The Lord's Prayer does indeed want to see the kingdom of God appear, but it is a much broader, richer concept of an invisible kingdom that seeps into every corner of our world, much as yeast causes dough to rise. For a potential Donewith, slogans such as making heaven more crowded are likely to be the final straw.

Local Churches, Changing Nations

This is an ambitious motto. This church sign, affiliated to a larger organization, wants to go large. Not content with simply being a local church in one locality, it seeks to transform an entire nation! This might sound like an inspirational rallying cry for a crusade that will change society, although it offers no clue as to what this change might look like. The emphasis could be interpreted as a major project that its members are called to sign up for. The assumption seems to be that the church, for all its flaws, is God's chosen instrument to bring about change. Is the church therefore the vehicle by which the kingdom is brought to fruition? For those who are beginning to ask questions about their level of church involvement, this motto could be a step too far and it certainly sounds very exhausting. Many people have enough difficulty changing their own lives, let alone a whole nation.

Building a Community of Grace

This motto has an unusual feel to it. There is the hint of provisionality about it. The work of this church is unfinished, it is still being constructed and perhaps it will never be. But why the word 'building'? This sounds like a construction site with men in hard hats and diggers. It has a rough feel to it. Why did this church not use verbs like nurturing or growing when describing what it is attempting to do? And what is the nature of this building? It is all about community, a family that is knit together and functions as an integrated, balanced constellation of relationships. At least that is the ideal scenario. But, for some, communities can be unsafe places, where there is jostling and pushing and shoving going on.

The hallmark of this community, however, is grace, yet this depiction is also ambiguous. Does it mean that the community itself is characterized by grace in the way that it functions? Or does it mean that this community is the recipient of the grace of God? Something unearned, perhaps, or something that is given as the result of strenuous effort? Maybe this church wants to say that it is both the recipient of grace and the dispenser of grace simultaneously. Maybe the expression of grace by this community to the wider world is entirely the inevitable consequence of having been the recipients of grace in the first place. None of these questions are answered, but are left open ended for a multiplicity of possible responses. It is an enigmatic motto. For someone tiptoeing around the edge of church, I suspect that this might be a more accommodating community for them to belong to.

4 What Are the Issues at Stake?

Some years ago, the well-known developmental psychologist, Erik Erikson, put forward a theory that at every stage of our lives there are issues within each of us that need to be resolved in order for us to develop into healthy functioning adults.[10] For the newborn child the issues centre around trust versus mistrust; for the adult between the ages of 18–40, the polarities deal with questions of intimacy versus isolation. Whilst this may be somewhat contrived and the age groups are not necessarily set in stone, the idea of needing to resolve sets of tensions is a very useful one. In a similar way, the Donewiths find themselves grappling with a series of conundrums for which they seek resolution. Those people interviewed for this study decided to leave church after perhaps a lifetime of membership. They did so for a whole variety of reasons, as we have seen in chapter two. But underneath the list of specific issues that the Donewiths found so troublesome lie deeply felt longings. This chapter will attempt to bring those out into the light of day.

Belonging versus Detachment

One issue that those interviewed referred to was being required to commit time, money, effort and goods to projects. At times these were projects or initiatives that they did not want to invest time and energy in yet felt pressure to do so. The problem then came more clearly into focus. How can I belong to a community of people if I do not fully resonate with their values and priorities? Is it possible to belong partially, hanging on by the fingertips? Maybe there is a looser way of belonging within the body of Christ. Do I have to be compliant and play by the unspoken rules of this particular church, or is it safe to be true to myself and ask the questions that I want to ask and articulate the very real doubts that I may have? For some, the experience of trying to belong to a church community in which there may be difficult and abrasive people becomes simply too much of an effort. If this is a voluntary activity, they ask themselves, why am I spending my free time struggling to be pleasant to church people who, if truth be told, I simply do not like?

The felt need to belong, however, is a natural human instinct. Attachment theory asserts that seeking a secure attachment that nourishes and protects is not only our primary task as newborns but our lifelong task too. Belonging to a church is a distinct form of attachment and can take a huge variety of manifestations. Those people who have decided to disengage from one form of commitment to church life often seek an alternative mode of belonging—one that meets their needs at their particular stage of life. What was a nourishing experience at one time is no longer. Maybe their circumstances have changed, the demands upon their time and money have altered or maybe the distinctive flavour of the church to which they had hitherto belonged has metamorphosed as well. Whatever the range of causes the sense of dissonance becomes too acute to tolerate and then question marks about belonging come flooding in.

Some people leave their churches only to discover a sense of belonging in a dispersed church, such as the one found at the Northumbria Community with its mother house called Nether Springs. Such communities do not meet together each week, but they share a strong sense of community through their Rule of Life. The attraction is the absence of any emphasis on hierarchy or conformity but rather the explicit and gentle message of accompanying one another on a journey of faith. Others choose to belong in a more anonymous fashion, as has already been mentioned, by attending a cathedral where few demands are placed on them to form new friendships or participate in projects. They can slip in at the back of the building unnoticed and quietly slip away afterwards. The rhythm of the liturgy is enough perhaps to offer spiritual nourishment.

Mystery versus Certainty

Barbara Brown Taylor, who stimulated the discussion in this booklet at the outset, has written eloquently about her journey towards ordination and her subsequent journey out of the church in her book, *Leaving Church*.[11] She writes about the mysterious, sacred power of beholding.

> The parts of the Christian story that had drawn me into the church were not the believing parts but the beholding parts
>
> - Behold I bring you good tidings of great joy
> - Behold the lamb of God
> - Behold I stand at the door and knock
>
> Whether the narratives starred hayseed shepherds confronted by hosts of glittering angels or desert pilgrims watching something like a dove descend upon a man in a river as a voice from heaven called him beloved, Christian faith seems to depend on beholding things that were clearly beyond belief.

What Barbara Brown Taylor expresses here is that she was drawn into faith, not because she was outsmarted by someone well trained in Christian apologetics, but by experiencing something ineffable that could not be contained, let alone defined precisely. It was the sense of awe and wonder that the psalmist tries to capture when he says, 'Taste and see that the Lord is good' (Ps 34.8). It is in the act of tasting that faith comes alive, the ingesting of the bread of life, the drinking from the eternal spring. This is the stuff of faith and Donewiths long for this like a thirsty traveller in the desert. And whenever faith is reduced to defending orthodoxy or prescriptive how-to behaviours, then the Donewiths quietly withdraw and say to themselves, 'This is not for me.' Mystery and certainty are not necessarily in opposition to each other. It is the insistence on certain types of certainty and the perceived mistrust of mystery that some find difficult to stomach. For those on the edge of church there is a longing for a less assertive articulation of faith combined with plenty of room for untidy questions to be asked. To quote Barbara Brown Taylor once more:

> I wanted out of the belief business and back into the beholding business. I wanted to recover the kind of faith that has nothing to do with being sure what I believe and everything to do with trusting God to catch me though I am not sure of anything.

Faith that is filled with mystery is a sensual, felt experience. This kind of faith requires verbs such as tasting, seeing, drinking, eating and touching to be deployed, verbs that bring to life something of the essence of the faith journey. And this is where the importance of language becomes evident. Some churches place great emphasis on depictions of God in strong absolutes such as sovereign Lord, the one who is omniscient and in full and absolute control. Whilst it might be possible to justify the use of such language using biblical proof texts, for those who are Donewiths, it is the more nuanced, softer descriptors that allow for a greater openness to exploration and enquiry. If God is described, by way of example, as the one who comes alongside (the Holy Spirit) or the one who shelters us under the shadow of his wings, then such terms sound more invitational and less imbued with demand or certainty. The use of language therefore depends on tone as well as the priority of emphasis. Language has the capacity both to open up and also to shut down.

Identity versus Performance

Churches can often be busy places. There are always jobs to be done, tea to be made, children to be inspired and the poor to be fed. The neediness of the world around us is never ending. It is not surprising therefore that churches want to meet this need and to be salt and light to their neighbourhoods. The danger is, however, as the Donewiths can sense, that it gives the impression that this is what the life of faith amounts to. One long list of things to do, leading perhaps—for some—to compassion fatigue. What some Donewiths long for in their spiritual journey is to discover more of their truest identity. Who is the real me underneath all this activity? What does God really think of me? How can I love my neighbour as myself when I am not even sure who myself is? And so this is the tussle: to give oneself enough space and enough time to know who I am before God. Maybe this is exactly what St Paul was praying for when he wrote, 'I pray that you, being rooted and established in love, may have power, together with all the Lord's holy people, to grasp how wide and long and high and deep is the love of Christ, and to know this love that surpasses knowledge'(Eph 3.17–19).

In his book, *The Forgotten Father,* Tom Smail makes the point that the entire ministry of Jesus stemmed from his profound sense of identity as the Son of the Father.[12] This was his core identity and everything flowed from this. His stories, his encounters along the way, his miracles, his convictions, his courage and his compassion, all of it emanated from his ontological status as the Son. It is this priority of knowing his identity that preceded any action of his. Lurking underneath the feeling of disconnect that Donewiths experience is the longing to discover more of their own identity as human beings in a complex world and as hesitant, stumbling followers of Jesus. When churches pay more attention to what we do than who we are, when they become absorbed with function rather than learning how to belong together, then those who struggle with the church find themselves looking for the exit door.

Donewiths long to discover more of their identity as stumbling followers of Jesus

Exploration versus Exhortation

Those who have spent much of their lives in churches have grown used to exhortations. Each Sunday they hear passionate messages urging them to confess more, to pray more, to give more, to love more...whatever it is you have been doing, do more of it. The messages come laced with an implicit warning, namely that this is the only way in which one can experience more of the grace of God. Over time these exhortations have begun to sound like conditional statements. God is willing to dispense his grace only if certain prior conditions have been met. Grace does not come cheaply, you have been told over and over again. You have to prove you are serious with God before he will do anything at all. At times even the 24/7 prayer movement has begun to feel like a mass exercise in divine arm twisting.

What the Donewiths find themselves longing for, however, is the freedom to explore. For them it feels as if the church has domesticated God and made God fit rather too comfortably in some odd-looking cardboard box. These committed church members now long for the freedom to be astonished by an unscripted encounter with an undomesticated God. Maybe God can be discovered in all sorts of unusual places, within the lives of those who have not prayed or served in the way you have all your life. A life of exploration is filled with words like 'maybe' and 'perhaps' and sentences that begin with 'I wonder...'

I suspect that many of the so-called Donewiths are not Donewiths at all. Rather, they feel that they are only just beginning on a new and exciting journey of adventure. The only requirement for this adventurous journey—maybe requirement is the wrong word—is an insistence on authenticity. All honest questions are welcomed, doubts can be freely expressed, being truly oneself is to be honoured and celebrated. Collecting together the broken, fragmented shards of one's humanity is an essential part of this way of discovering a true spirituality. This is what the Donewiths are seeking, a bit of breathing space away from those urgent exhortations to allow for an authentic spiritual journey to take place.

The Donewiths might also be sensing something else beneath the culture of exhortation, something perhaps harder to articulate. It the presence of a fearfulness. The fear is concerned with being a disappointment to God, or the fear of missing out on some promised blessing or even the fear of crossing a line from the safety of orthodox belief to the danger of perceived heresy. There is such a thing as a holy fear, however. It is frequently spoken of in the psalms and perhaps most vividly illustrated in the story of the transfiguration in the gospels. This kind of fear leaves one without words, for the presence of the sacred lies so heavily and beautifully all around. But the fear that the Donewiths sense in their churches is of an altogether different kind. It feels more like a cringing before God than a holy falling to the ground. It is more subservient than intimate. And sadly it is easy for churches to replace holy awe with fearful cringe as a tool of control.

Donewiths also sense the presence of fearfulness

The biblical scholar, Walter Brueggemann, in his magnum opus, *Theology of the Old Testament,* writes about the kaleidoscope of testimonies within the Jewish tradition concerning the nature of Yahweh.[13] At times God communicates his utter, unshakeable, dependable faithfulness, his *hesed,* towards his people. And at other times the witness of Israel concerns Yahweh's oddness, his utter unpredictability. These opposing character descriptors are never fully resolved and there appears to be no attempt to do so. God is who he is, present in the heart of everything but his edges cannot be delineated, his actions cannot be predicted. All we are invited to do is surrender ourselves to this passionate, wild, trustworthy divine reality. Old Testament witness to the character of

God is filled throughout with paradox and apparent contradiction. Yet over the centuries the Jews had learned to live with paradox without letting go of either end. Those who start tiptoeing out of the church through the back door long to explore this God, and are increasingly less interested in the God the church has seemingly tried to tame. If there is a place for exhortation it lies in such phrases as 'come and see…' The writer of the Letter to the Hebrews depicts this kind of adventurous faith in the story of Abraham and Sarah. 'By faith Abraham, when called to go to a place he would later receive as his inheritance, obeyed and went, even though he did not know where he was going' (Heb 11.8). Some Donewiths may have no idea where they are going; all they know is they want an adventure.

5 Is Donewiths the Right Term?

Throughout this booklet we have referred to those who have left the church rather flippantly as the 'Donewiths.' It is now time to revisit that term in order to ask if it really is the most compassionate and accurate way to describe them. The trouble with labels is that they have the capacity to categorize, to pigeonhole, and to collect together in one undifferentiated lump a disparate group of people who have their own personal stories to tell which are unique to them. To give them a collective name can sound pejorative and judgmental. This is precisely the mood that they have chosen to flee from. Some of those interviewed did use this phrase to depict themselves, for they felt that they were done with congregational and institutional expressions of church. None of them expressed any desire to form a new denomination or to have any new label attached to them.

This chapter will attempt to draw out the emotional journey that those who have left the church have taken and to ask if there is an alternative, gentler way of depicting their story.

Elizabeth Kubler-Ross's work on the stages of dealing with the loss of a loved one is well known. She writes about the way in which bereavement is such a complex process, oscillating between rage and sadness, bargaining and acceptance. It is not a linear path and can take many years to be fully completed. In a similar way, leaving church arouses a range of strong feelings. Let us explore what some of them might be.

Blame

Some people who leave church have absolutely no intention of ever stepping inside the door of any church again. They are angry that they have been hurt by the church and that the church has not delivered for them what they had hoped for. For such people leaving church has a full stop rather than a comma after it.

Relief

Initially the decision to finally leave a church that one has been a part of for much of our lives can feel like a relief. At long last the tedium of the weekly same-old, same-old has been left behind. No more midweek meetings, no more wrangling about who sits where, no more fundraising committees, no more internal squabbling. What a relief that it is all over! The sense of relief highlights the burden that such a form of belonging has become. Over the years being part of a church has become a source of chronic stress, which has taken its toll.

Grief

At some stage in the process of leaving, feelings of grief may come flooding in. Grief at the loss of community, grief at the absence of friends with whom you may have shared significant life events, grief at the loss of a role that you may have played at one stage in your life which you and others had valued. All this is now gone and inevitably the vacuum that remains is palpable.

Disappointment

For some, the sensation of disappointment is one of the hardest reactions to bear. Earlier in one's life, fulfilling an apparent God-given calling felt noble and sacred. Christ calls us to create a new community on Earth, one which radiates the love of Christ and transforms society. You have been caught up in this vision and have given time, money and prayer to making it a visible reality. Yet over the years what has eaten away at your soul is the absence of gentleness. The church has become for you sharp-edged and demanding. The promised land seems as far away as ever and you feel there are only so many years that you can keep going, hoping, longing, striving to see some glimpse of the kingdom of God arriving. Eventually such yearnings metamorphose into disappointment and you leave the church with only distant memories.

Disorientation

One of those interviewed told of how leaving church required a period of adjustment to a new weekly rhythm. This was profoundly disorientating. What do we do now on Sunday mornings? What shall we do on Wednesday evenings? Who are our friends now? Are there any other people who feel like us? Do we want to belong anywhere? Will I ever fit in with the feelings and questions that I have? And what exactly do I believe these days about the Nicene Creed? Am I still orthodox and does that even matter to me anymore? Such questions are profoundly disorientating and may require a considerable period of deconstruction of long-held paradigms of perception before any rebuilding can take place.

Reconfiguring

At some stage in the process of leaving church some reconfiguring may take place. Have we actually left the Christian church altogether or are we simply searching for another way to be church? Canon Dr George Lings—the former Church Army researcher into the fresh expressions movement—puts it like this when describing his own situation:

> I would not say that I am now unchurched or dechurched but re-churched.

In conversation with George Lings, he makes the honest and entirely non-judgmental observation that for him, at his stage of life, being part of a local congregation is no longer appropriate. Instead he has found alternative ways of belonging. He has in effect been rechurched. I suspect that these sentiments could be echoed by others who have left church as they have known it and now look for new expressions of corporate life. Such people are not Donewiths. They are simply finding ways by which they can be rechurched.

Dispersed Community

One of those expressions of church already mentioned is the dispersed Northumbria Community. This community places itself firmly within the Celtic tradition, which can trace its history back many hundreds of years to its inception in Ireland. Celtic Christianity is much more rooted in a non-hierarchical form of governance and draws heavily upon finding God in creation.

The Northumbria Community requires its members to commit to a simple rule of life. This rule is defined in terms of being available to God and others from within the cell of our own hearts and being intentionally and deliberately vulnerable. It asks three simple yet profound questions to those who choose to join them.

- Who is it that you seek?
- How then shall we live?
- How should we sing the Lord's song in a foreign land?

These questions may be asked in a small group setting or may be addressed privately. And they may be asked time and again, for the answers will vary depending on our context, our mood and even the time of day. The questions are intended to invite and inspire reflection rather than to cajole. There are no correct answers, simply provisional responses from those who have set out on the journey. Some have called this kind of church an expression of new monasticism; others may find such labels unnecessary. The openness of this kind of expression of church is not vacuous. It is filled with content and rooted in biblical story.

Spiritual Stages

Another possible way of delineating what is actually going on with those who choose to *leave the church* they have known for years is offered by Brian D McLaren in his book *Naked Spirituality.*[14] McLaren suggests that the spiritual journey that many people take through the course of their lives can be marked by four seasons: simplicity, complexity, perplexity and harmony. Those who have left the church may well be able to recognize such facets in their own faith. There may have been times when faith was held in a simple, almost childlike way, when being part of a believing community brought only nourishment and joy. At some point, however, this simplicity was disturbed by painful experiences in life that went unexplained or were inadequately processed. The sheer complexity of life itself seemed to fit poorly in the faith container that their church offered them. Inevitably this leads to a period of huge confusion and perplexity. What kind of faith can I now possess with any degree of integrity? The fourth term, harmony, may refer to a place of *shalom* that is eventually discovered once the reconfiguring process has been undertaken. Alternatively it could also be true that these four words do not necessarily describe a neat linear progression of faith; rather, they describe elements of faith that are always present and which need to be constantly negotiated.

6 Conclusion

The intention of this listening exercise has been to understand as deeply as possible what happens when someone chooses to take what, for them, is a brand new path of belonging. It is not the intention to pass judgment either on the churches that some have departed from, nor upon those who have left their churches behind. Unavoidably this has shone a spotlight on some aspects of church life that some—maybe even many—find troublesome and painful. Being a community of faith is a precarious business. No one group gets it completely right all the time and, as George Lings affirmed in his interview, there is surely still a place for the various institutions of the church in God's gracious hand. After all, the New Testament is actually a witness to multiple dysfunctional communities, each of which struggled to find a way to express the reality and joy of the kingdom of God that had come. Those who have left the church—the Donewiths, if you will—have much to teach us if we have ears to listen.

We will leave the final word with Brian McLaren. Writing for the Centre for Action and Contemplation, he sets out a vision for a diverse and decentralized movement:

> It will not be anti-institutional because institutions are necessary for human survival, but neither will it be institutional, in the sense that it is pre-occupied with its own survival or bringing benefits only to its members…I can imagine hundreds of thousands of congregations… each a locally and globally engaged school of love, teaching future generations to discover, practise and live in love: love for our neighbour, love for ourselves, love for all creatures and all creation—all comprising love for God, who is all in all in all.[15]

For Further Reading

Steve Aisthorpe, *The Invisible Church* (Edinburgh: Saint Andrew Press, 2016)

Grace Davie, *Religion in Britain Since 1945: Believing Without Belonging* (Oxford: Blackwell, 1994)

Michael Fanstone, *The Sheep That Got Away* (Oxford: Lion Hudson, 1993)

William D Hendricks, *Exit Interviews* (Chicago, IL: Moody Press, 1993)

Brian McLaren, *Naked Spirituality* (London: Hodder and Stoughton, 2011)

Josh Packard and Ashleigh Hope, *Church Refugees* (Loveland, CO: Group Publishing, 2015)

Tom Smail, *The Forgotten Father* (Eugene, OR: Wipf and Stock, 2001)

Barbara Brown Taylor, *Leaving Church: A Memoir of Faith* (San Francisco, CA: HarperOne, 2016)

William Paul Young, *The Shack* (London: Hodder and Stoughton, 2007)

Notes

1 Michael Fanstone, *The Sheep That Got Away* (Oxford: Lion Hudson, 1993).

2 Steve Aisthorpe, *The Invisible Church* (Edinburgh: St Andrew Press, 2016).

3 Bill Plotkin, *Soulcraft: Crossing into the Mysteries of Nature and Psyche* (New World Library, 2003).

4 Tim Chester, *A Meal with Jesus: Discovering Grace, Community and Mission Around the Table* (Wheaton, IL: Crossway Books, 2011).

5 Francis Chan, *Letters to the Church* (Colorado Springs, CO: David C Cook, 2018).

6 Martin Lloyd-Jones, *Reflections: A Treasury of Daily Readings* (Nelson Bibles, 1995).

7 John Packard and Ashleigh Hope, *Church Refugees* (Loveland, CO: Group Publishing, 2015).

8 Leslie Francis and Philip J Richter, *Gone for Good* (Norwich: Epworth Press, 2007).

9 William P Young, *The Shack* (London: Hodder and Stoughton, 2007).

10 Stephanie Scheck, *The Stages of Psychosocial Development According to Erik H Erikson* (GRIN Verlag, 2014).

11 Barbara Brown Taylor, *Leaving Church* (Norwich: Canterbury Press, 2016).

12 Tom Smail, *The Forgotten Father* (London: Hodder and Stoughton, 1990).

13 Walter Brueggemann, *Theology of the Old Testament* (Minneapolis, MN: Augsburg Fortress, 1997).

14 Brian D McLaren, *Naked Spirituality* (London: Hodder and Stoughton, 2011).

15 Brian McLaren in *Daily Meditations*, Centre for Action and Contemplation, 3 January 2020.